Our Code of Ethics

"Life will bring you pain all by itself. Your responsibility is to create joy."
- Milton Erickson

Our Code of Ethics | ISBN: 978-80-87518-09-0

Welcome!

We value your trust, and we're here to make sure you get the most out of your experience with our therapy / coaching services.

Let us know of any question, concern or suggestion you may have:

"It may be hard for an egg to turn into a bird: it would be a jolly sight harder for it to learn to fly while remaining an egg. We are like eggs at present. And you cannot go on indefinitely being just an ordinary, decent egg. We must be hatched or go bad."

- C.S. Lewis

Contents

"Do the right thing. It will gratify some people and astonish the rest."

- Mark Twain

I. Basic Responsibilities

Our therapists and coaches support client welfare and rights, and the ethical and constructive use of their services. When clients are not physically present during sessions, as in phone sessions, Our therapists and coaches take extra measures to meet their responsibilities to clients as needed.

1. Our therapists and coaches support non-discrimination, and provide equal consideration regardless of race, gender, religion, national origin, age, sexual orientation, disability, socioeconomic, or marital status. Our therapists and coaches take reasonable measures to accommodate clients with physical disabilities.

2. Our therapists and coaches understand that their clients trust them, and so they refrain from exploiting that trust. They also understand that dual relationships can become more complicated than expected and result in bad outcomes or the perception of an ethical breach. Our therapists and coaches avoid

creating any relationships with their clients that are at all likely to impair their judgment or tempt them to exploit the client. This is especially important where there are ongoing sessions, as opposed to one or a few sessions that are not highly personal.

3. It is questionable to have a "dual relationship," meaning one in which the practitioner and client engage in a different relationship at the same time, such as by also being business partners. Before considering an additional relationship, the practitioner should allow a reasonable amount of time to elapse after the sessions are complete.

When you cannot avoid a dual relationship, as may occur in a small town, the practitioner will take precautions and create limits for that relationship to ensure that they maintain good judgment and refrain from any exploitation. In any case, sex and dating are inadvisable when in a practitioner-client relationship, and for a reasonable amount of time afterwards.

Where there is significant likelihood of a dual relationship, the practitioner will consider referring the person to another practitioner.

Examples of dual relationship actions include borrowing money, hiring, engaging in a business venture with, or engaging in a close personal relationship with a client. This may also apply to the client's spouse, partner or family members.

4. Our therapists and coaches honor their professional commitment to clients. This includes refraining from abandoning or neglecting clients whose sessions are not complete. To this end, Our therapists and coaches maintain procedures to support this, such as providing contact information and instructions as to what to do in case of an emergency or in case the therapist / coach is away, and by terminating sessions properly. This should include a professional will with instructions as to how to transfer, maintain or properly dispose of any confidential or important records.

5. Our therapists and coaches stop seeing clients for appropriate reasons only, and do so in an ethical manner. These reasons may include the client not benefiting adequately, there is not a good reason to continue, the therapist / coach is experiencing some kind of impairment such

as mental illness, or the relationship has developed a significant ethical problem. for clinically sound reasons and in an appropriate manner. When ending sessions, the therapist / coach makes sure that any referrals for services or other arrangements are made promptly.

6. Our therapists and coaches do not continue sessions with clients purely for their own financial gain, but it is ethical to discontinue when fees are not paid.

7. Our therapists and coaches are not gurus, and are not adamant about any advice they offer except where safety and emergencies are concerned. Our therapists and coaches respect the right of their clients to make their own decisions in all areas of their lives, including personal relationships. At the same time, the practitioner will help clients understand the consequences of their decisions, and will give them enough information that clients can make informed decisions about therapy / coaching. This information includes the potential risks and benefits of therapy / coaching based on the client's situation and capacities.

8. Our therapists and coaches inform clients all key policies in advance. These include the

extent of their availability for emergencies and for other contacts between sessions, as well as issues such as fees, no show charges and other fee-related policies. These include whether extended sessions cost more, and how the client will be enabled to decide on whether to accept an extended session.

9. Our therapists and coaches obtain written consent before making any kind of media recording of sessions. The consent will include the conditions in which the recording can be played and who will experience it.

10. Our therapists and coaches will explain to their client that the content of their sessions will be kept confidential, and the practitioner will honor this into perpetuity. In the event of a court order or safety issue, the practitioner is not required to maintain confidentiality. The client should understand this in advance.

11. Our therapists and coaches inform clients of their qualifications and experience prior to providing services. This can be in the form of a written summary.

12. If there are to be electronic communications, Our therapists and coaches inform their clients

of the potential risks to confidentiality, what to do if there is no response (there may have been a technical problem) and how emergencies communicated electronically will be handled.

13. If the client sees another practitioner of some kind, such as a mental health provider, the therapist / coach will provide all useful information when requested by the client. The practitioner will not withhold this information because fees have not been paid. The therapist / coach will collaborate with practitioners as needed for the welfare of the client, when given permission by the client.

II. Scope of Practice and Referrals

Our therapists and coaches do not work with clients who have problems that the practitioner does not have qualifications and skills to work with, and they refer to appropriate professionals as needed.

1. The therapist / coach will refer clients to appropriate medical or psychotherapy treatment providers when there is a concern that assessment or treatment of symptoms of medical or mental disorders may be needed.

2. The therapist / coach is as aware of the limits of his or her skills as they are of their abilities. This is called scope of practice. As a result, the practitioner prevents harm by knowing when and how to refer clients for treatment of possible medical or psychological disorders.

3. The therapist / coach learns to recognize symptoms that may indicate medical and

psychological disorders so that they will be effective and timely in making referrals.

III. Confidentiality

Our therapists and coaches take their clients' privacy seriously. They understand that clients may divulge personal information that they would not want shared with anyone else. Personal information can harm peoples' careers, relationships, and other important life areas. Except for urgent safety concerns, therapists and coaches do not make moral decisions that would lead them to violate the privacy of their clients, and they never indulge in gossip. Practitioners have unique confidentiality responsibilities because the "patient" in a therapeutic relationship may be more than one person. The overriding principle is that Our therapists and coaches respect the confidences of their patient(s).

1. Our therapists and coaches are best known for providing coaching that enhances success and well being, and do not treat mental illnesses, therefore, so long as no coercion is involved, the practitioner may solicit permission to use client's recommendations and names in

communications and advertising, and in teaching or presenting. The client must clearly understand the potential consequences and nature of the use of their name, and give permission in advance and in writing on a form that includes this information. This can prevent serious misunderstandings later. The therapist / coach avoids this practice if there is any doubt about the client's objectivity, such as occurs if the client feels dependent upon the therapist / coach or confers authority to the therapist / coach in some manner.

2. Our therapists and coaches maintain the total privacy of their clients, including their names or any information that could identify them. The only exceptions to this are a) any legal requirements, such as a court order, b) the need to use specific information to defend themselves in a court action (and the release of information is limited to what is necessary only), c) as needed in order to pursue fees in a legal action (and this is limited to the name of the client, the dates of the sessions, the amount owed, a signed form showing that the client has agreed to fees or policies but that does not contain information about the client's problems,

and the service provided, d) as permitted by the client.

3. Our therapists and coaches maintain client records in a safe and secure manner. They are aware of the risks and limitations of any technology used, and take appropriate steps to prevent breaches. They take extra cautions when transmitting or receiving client information. They dispose of records, including any hardware containing them, such as computer memory devices, in a manner that fully protects confidentiality.

4. Our therapists and coaches ensure that their employees, contractors or other personnel maintain confidentiality, and that they only have access to information that is necessary for the conduct of business and in a manner that the client understands and accepts.

IV. Professional Competence and Integrity

Our therapists and coaches maintain high standards of professional competence and integrity.

1. Our therapists and coaches maintain records of their sessions as needed for competent practice, for maintenance of any signed agreements, for reference in case there is a time lag between sessions, for consulting with other helping professionals, billing, and for any other purposes as needed.

2. Our therapists and coaches seek professional assistance as needed for any problems that may interfere with their performance or judgment.

3. Our therapists and coaches as teachers or presenters, present accurate information from reputable sources.

4. Our therapists and coaches develop the understanding necessary to work with people of other cultures. The identify the cultural and

ethnic background and related needs of their clients so that they may provide effective services.

5. Our therapists and coaches stay up-to-date in their field through ongoing educational experiences. They also get ongoing continuing education that expands their knowledge pertaining to psychology and health, because of the diverse issues that clients bring.

6. Our therapists and coaches maintain a reputation for honesty, fairness and ethics in their lives. They refrain from any kind of harassment, exploitation or illegal activity.

7. Our therapists and coaches do not provide any services that are outside of their abilities and legal scope of practice. Unless qualified and legally sanctioned, Our therapists and coaches do not treat or offer to treat mental or physical illnesses. While people may improve in these areas as a result of therapy / coaching, the practitioner does not promote his or her services as a form of treatment. Promoted services may include training on therapy / coaching, including self-therapy / coaching, stress management, coaching, and stress

management, (barring any legal or ethical concerns).

8. Our therapists and coaches make sure that any new types of clients they see or skills they use are appropriate from a legal and ethical point of view, and will be performed competently as a result of having the proper training, supervision, consultation or experience as needed.

9. Our therapists and coaches do not provide services that will conflict with a person's psychotherapy. The practitioner uses special caution and consideration with a potential client who is receiving psychotherapy. This is because the person may have a mental disorder that places special needs upon any relationship that may result in focusing on memories or goals, or that may induce emotional awareness or deep relaxation. Generally, the practitioner is advised to consult with the psychotherapist before starting sessions. It may be appropriate to proceed when the client is fully able to indicate that they are stable and can tolerate the activities listed in this section, such as experiencing increased awareness.

10. Our therapists and coaches take reasonable steps to prevent the distortion or misuse of their approach and knowledge, particularly by the media and influential persons. This includes steps such as letters to the editor, personal communications, and collective communication from practitioners.

11. Our therapists and coaches want to affect people and their community in the most positive way possible, and they want to generate and preserve respect for their approach, so they exercise care in their public statements, live or in any medium. As part of their ongoing education, Our therapists and coaches learn how to recognize and engage in rational and ethical rhetoric, debate and public discourse. This includes understanding and avoiding logical fallacies.

12. Our therapists and coaches only engage in research when they have adequate support, skills and knowledge to do so. Our therapists and coaches do not make public statements as to the results of their research unless they are adequately trained and competent to carry out reliable research. Our therapists and coaches gain the knowledge pertaining to research, and

will only talk about the results of others' research when they can do so competently and credibly.

V. Responsibility to Students

As with clients, Our therapists and coaches do not exploit the trust of their students.

1. Our therapists and coaches apply the ethical guidelines in their conduct with students as with clients. This refers to exploitation, dual relationships that may impair judgment, sexual contact, and sexual harassment.

2. Our therapists and coaches take reasonable measures to prevent their students from holding themselves out as able to perform services and skills that are beyond their actual skills and experience. This is reflected in the standards and testing related to any certifications or references provided.

4.3 Our therapists and coaches who act as teachers or who supervise students that are gaining experience maintain and enhance their teaching or supervision skills, and get consultation as needed.

VI. Responsibility to Colleagues and Other Professionals

Our therapists and coaches treat colleagues and other professionals with courtesy, respect and fairness. They cooperate with their colleagues in order to support the well being of their clients and community.

1. Our therapists and coaches respect their colleagues privacy, and maintain any confidences that their colleagues share with them, except where a clear ethical or legal need requires disclosure.

2. Our therapists and coaches make reasonable efforts to help colleagues who are impaired by problems such as substance abuse or mental illness.

VII. Responsibility to Therapy / Coaching

Our therapists and coaches work to advance the goals of therapy / coaching and respect for the professionals involved in therapy / coaching.

1. Our therapists and coaches continue to act in accordance with the ethics of their profession, without being compromised by their employment or membership in an organization.

2. Our therapists and coaches give credit to people who contribute to their publications in proportion to the contribution and according to traditional publication practices. This includes giving attribution to the people who came up with original ideas and contributions.

3. Our therapists and coaches take responsibility for the marketing and promotion of their work, training offerings, and publications, ensuring that it is done accurately and honestly.

4. Our therapists and coaches recognize the importance of contributing to a better community and society. They engage in practices that support this, such as devoting a portion of their professional activity to services for which there is little or no financial return.

5. Our therapists and coaches recognize the importance of supporting laws and regulations that pertain to therapy / coaching and that serve the public interest, and of fighting or altering laws and regulations that do not.

VIII. Responsibility to the Legal System

Our therapists and coaches recognize and understand their role in the legal system and their duty to remain objective and honest.

1. Our therapists and coaches who have questions or concerns about a case or practice that may have legal repercussions consult a qualified attorney in order to ensure that their conduct is in compliance with the law. They never assume that they know the law through using common sense, their impression of what is fair, or information that is not from a legal authority or that they do not fully understand.

2. Our therapists and coaches who give testimony in legal proceedings testify truthfully and avoid making misleading statements.

3. Our therapists and coaches understand laws that have a bearing upon their practices, directly or indirectly, and comply with those laws.

4. Our therapists and coaches do not publicly express professional opinions about an individual's mental or emotional condition, unless they clearly state the limitations of their knowledge of the situation and that they are offering a personal opinion. This is to help ensure legally appropriate testimony, and to avoid making statements that may legally compromise the practitioner or other people.

IX. Financial Arrangements

Our therapists and coaches make financial arrangements with clients and students that are understandable, and conform to accepted professional practices and legal requirements.

1. Our therapists and coaches do not offer or accept payment for referrals. This prevents a loss of objectivity in making referrals that could exploit and bring harm to clients or divert them from a more appropriate referral.

2. Our therapists and coaches do not financially exploit their clients.

3. Our therapists and coaches disclose in advance their fees and how they will be computed. They make sure their clients understand matters such as charges for canceled or missed appointments and any interest to be charged on unpaid balances, at the beginning of treatment. They give reasonable notice of any changes in these policies or amounts.

4. Our therapists and coaches give reasonable notice to clients with unpaid balances of their intent to sue, or to refer for collection. Whenever legal action is taken, therapists will avoid disclosure of clients' personal information such as their problems. If the practitioner refers to a collection agency, they avoid disclosure of clinical information and select an ethical agency.

5. Our therapists and coaches normally don't accept non-monetary remuneration such as goods or services for their services. This is because it can create conflicts of interest and lead the client to feel exploited. This can harm the therapist-client relationship.

X. ADVERTISING

Our therapists and coaches enable potential clients to make informed choices regarding their services.

1. Our therapists and coaches are honest about the current nature of their skills, training and experience.

2. Our therapists and coaches advertise honestly.

3. Our therapists and coaches display their name, credentials and business name in a way that does not mislead potential clients in any way or create any unjustified expectation.

4. Our therapists and coaches correct, wherever possible, false, misleading, or inaccurate information about their qualifications, services, or products.

5. Our therapists and coaches use great care in using any testimonials in a manner that is in compliance with their existing agreement with the client or ex-client, and refrain from soliciting

or using testimonials in any way that interferes with the best interests of that person.

6. Our therapists and coaches don't use unqualified or other initials after their names to give the impression of a license or academic degree that they do not have.

www.ingramcontent.com/pod-product-compliance
Ingram Content Group UK Ltd.
Pitfield, Milton Keynes, MK11 3LW, UK
UKHW042002190726
13854UKWH00005B/2119

9 788087 518090